DATE DUE			

3 3721 00282728 7

977.1
J

Joseph, Paul.

Ohio

The United States

Ohio

Paul Joseph
ABDO & Daughters

visit us at
www.abdopub.com

Published by Abdo & Daughters, 4940 Viking Drive, Suite 622, Edina, Minnesota 55435.
Copyright © 1998 by Abdo Consulting Group, Inc., Pentagon Tower, P.O. Box 36036,
Minneapolis, Minnesota 55435 USA. International copyrights reserved in all countries.
No part of this book may be reproduced in any form without written permission from the
publisher.

Printed in the United States.

Cover and Interior Photo credits: Peter Arnold, Inc., SuperStock, Archive, Corbis-
Bettmann, Ohio Historical Society

Edited by Lori Kinstad Pupeza
Contributing editor Brooke Henderson
Special thanks to our Checkerboard Kids—Priscilla Cáceres, Grace Hansen,
Matthew Nichols

All statistics taken from the 1990 census; The Rand McNally Discovery Atlas of The
United States.

Library of Congress Cataloging-in-Publication Data

Joseph, Paul, 1970-
        Ohio / Paul Joseph
        p. cm. -- (United States)
        Includes index.
        Summary: Surveys the people, geography, and history of the state known as the
        "Buckeye State."
        ISBN 1-56239-870-9
        1. Ohio--Juvenile literature. [1. Ohio.] I. Title. II. Series: United States
        (Series)
        F491.3.J67 1998
        977.1--dc21   97-18681
                                                                                    CIP
                                                                                    AC

Contents

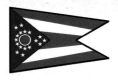

Welcome to Ohio

The wonderful state of Ohio is known as the Buckeye State. The popular nickname comes from the trees that were covering the state before the **settlers** arrived. **Native Americans** gave the trees the name "Buckeye" because the light spot in its brown seed resembled the eye of a buck, or, a male deer.

The nickname stuck, and today the Buckeye is the state tree. The state's name comes from a Native American word that means "beautiful river" or "large river."

People have been attracted to this wonderful state throughout history. Many famous people have called this state home. Ohio is sometimes called the Mother of Modern Presidents because seven presidents of the United States were born here.

The Ohio River passing through Cincinnati.

Fast Facts

OHIO
Capital and Largest city
Columbus (632,910 people)
Area
41,004 square miles
(106,200 sq km)
Population
10,887,325 people
Rank: 7th
Statehood
March 1, 1803
(17th state admitted)
Principal rivers
Ohio River
Scioto River
Highest point
Campbell Hill;
1,550 feet (472 m)
Motto
With God, all things are possible
Song
"Beautiful Ohio"
Famous People
Neil Armstrong, Thomas Edison,
John Glenn, Steven Spielberg

*S*tate Flag

*S*carlet Carnation

*C*ardinal

*B*uckeye

About Ohio

The Buckeye State

Detail area

Ohio's abbreviation

Borders: west (Indiana), north (Michigan, Lake Erie), east (Pennsylvania, West Virginia), south (West Virginia, Kentucky)

Nature's Treasures

Ohio has a great mixture of treasures in its state. Ohio has rolling hills, rich farmland, and **minerals** in the land. Lake Erie, along with other lakes and rivers, are also some of Ohio's treasures.

Long ago, **Native American** Mound Builders built huge mounds in the ground. The mounds were probably used for burial or ceremonies. Today, people visit the mounds.

There are more than one million acres of state parks, forests, and other outdoor areas that people of Ohio use. Even the larger cities have parks right in the city.

Water is one of Ohio's best treasures. Lake Erie sits to the north of the state. There, people use the beaches and water to swim, boat, and fish.

Under the state's ground are many **minerals**. The minerals most often found are coal, sandstone, clay, and crushed stone.

The sun setting on the Ohio River.

Beginnings

Before the Europeans began settling in Ohio, the **Native Americans** lived there. The first known people to live there were the Mound Builders. Later, the Erie Native Americans lived on the southern shore of Lake Erie.

When Europeans came to Ohio in the 1700s, they found many Native Americans. Some of the groups were the Miami, Shawnee, Ottawa, Wyandot, and Delaware.

Wars broke out between the Europeans and Native Americans over land. Native Americans were forced off their land until all of Ohio was in control by the European **settlers**.

France was the first European country to claim Ohio. In 1763, France gave the land to England. The

Ohio region was taken over by the United States in 1787 after the **American Revolution**.

Cities began springing up and people were moving to Ohio by the thousands. On March 1, 1803, Ohio became the 17th state.

An ancient mound in the shape of a serpent.

B.C. to 1700

Earliest Land and People

 Millions of years ago, during the Ice Age, Ohio was covered by a huge glacier of ice.

 The first known people to live in Ohio were the **Native American** Mound Builders. Mounds were made as far back as 600 B.C.

 Other Native Americans live in the area before it is taken over by Europeans in the 1700s.

Ohio

B.C. to 1700

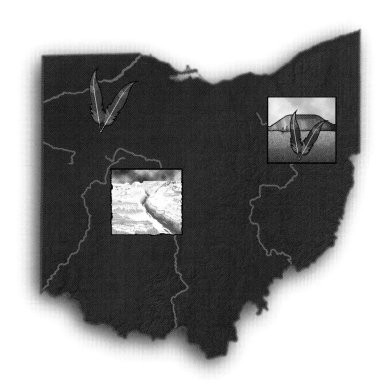

1600s to 1800s

Settlers to Statehood

 1670: Robert La Salle claims Ohio for France.

 1763: France gives Ohio to England in the Treaty of Paris.

 1803: Ohio becomes the 17th state on March 1.

Ohio

1600s to 1800s

1869 to Now

Historic People to Today

1869: Ulysses S. Grant becomes the first of seven people from Ohio to be elected president of the United States.

1903: The Wright brothers, from Dayton, Ohio, make the first airplane flight.

1937: The worst Ohio flood ever causes great damage to people and their homes.

1955: The Ohio Turnpike, a big highway, opens.

1990: The Cincinnati Reds baseball team win the World Series for the fifth time in a huge upset over the Oakland Athletics.

Ohio
1869 to Now

Ohio's People

There are almost 11 million people in the state of Ohio. Only six states have more people in them. However, 34 states are bigger in land size.

Throughout history, Ohio has had many famous people from its state. Ohio had seven men from its state elected president of the United States. The first was Ulysses S. Grant in 1869. Grant was born in Point Pleasant, Ohio in 1822. He was also a great Civil War leader.

The other six presidents were Rutherford B. Hayes, who became president in 1877, James A. Garfield in 1881, Benjamin Harrison in 1889, William McKinley in 1897, William Howard Taft in 1909, and Warren G. Harding in 1921.

Some may say that the two most famous people from Ohio were the Wright brothers. Orville and

Wilbur Wright grew up in Dayton, Ohio. As adults they worked together in bicycle shops, printing presses, and on newspapers in Dayton. What they really wanted to do was invent a flying machine. In 1903, the brothers became the first ever to fly an airplane.

Movie maker Steven Spielberg was born in Cincinnati, Ohio. He has made some of the most famous movies ever, like *Jaws*, *Raiders of the Lost Ark*, *E.T.*, *Jurassic Park*, and *Schindler's List*.

Ulysses S. Grant

Orville and Wilbur Wright

Steven Spielberg

Splendid Cities

Ohio has many splendid cities with many different things to do. The Buckeye State has six cities of more than 100,000 people. Only California, Florida, and Texas have more cities of this size.

Columbus is the capital of Ohio and has over 500,000 people living in it. It sits in the center of the state. The state has lots of iron and steel factories. Also located in the city is Ohio State University.

Cleveland is the other city with over 500,000 people living in it. Mills and factories turn out iron, steel, and other metal things. Cleveland sits on the shore of Lake Erie.

Cincinnati is a major port on the Ohio River. It is the site of a large

printing **industry**. It has many parks, the Cincinnati Zoo, and the University of Cincinnati.

Other cities in Ohio are Toledo at the western end of Lake Erie, Akron in the northeast, and Dayton in the southwest.

The Columbus Arts Festival in Columbus, Ohio.

Ohio's Land

From hills, to plains, to rivers and lakes, Ohio has it all. It is divided into three different areas.

The Allegheny Plateau region covers the entire eastern part of the state. It is a hilly area that has most of the state's forests. This region also has the richest **minerals**.

The Interior Plains area covers the middle, south, and western part of the state. This area is part of the great prairies of the central United States. This region has the highest point in the state—Campbell Hill.

The Lake Plains region follows the southern shore of

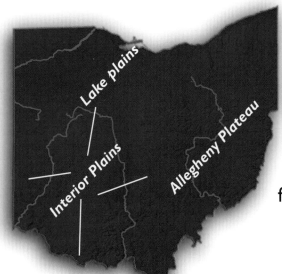

Lake Erie. There are areas of small hills in the region. Besides Lake Erie, there are many rivers in this region. They are the Muskingum, Hocking, Scioto, Little Miami, and Great Miami rivers.

The Cuyahoga National Recreation Area in Ohio.

Ohio at Play

The people of Ohio and Ohio's visitors have many fun things to do in the state. There are more than one million acres of state parks and forests.

Lake Erie has what some people call "vacationland." This is a strip of summer **resorts**, beaches, boating, and fishing areas. Thousands of people visit this place every summer.

The state's **Native American** mounds and its other historic attractions draw millions of visitors each year.

Some of the bigger cities have zoos filled with many kinds of animals. The best known in the state is the Cincinnati Zoo.

Professional teams like the Cincinnati Reds, Cleveland Indians, Cleveland Cavaliers, and Cincinnati Bengals play for all the sports fans in Ohio.

Ohio State University has one of the most consistently top-ranked college football teams in the nation. They have made it to the Rose Bowl many times. The University of Cincinnati is known for its fine basketball team, it is fun and exciting to watch.

The shore of Lake Erie is a popular tourist attraction.

Ohio at Work

The people of Ohio must work to make money. About one out of every four people in Ohio work in **manufacturing**. Most of these jobs can be found in the larger cities.

The biggest manufacturing **industry** in Ohio is making trucks. No other state builds more trucks than Ohio.

Many people in Ohio are farmers. The main **crops** that farmers grow there are corn, soybeans, hay, wheat, and oats. Farmers in Ohio also raise **cattle**, hogs, and sheep.

Because of the **minerals** in Ohio's ground, lots of people work at mines. Most of Ohio's **miners** work in coal mines. Others mine sandstone, clay, crushed stone, and gravel.

A lot of people work in **tourism.** People work in restaurants, stores, hotels, or **resorts**. They serve the people that visit Ohio.

The people of Ohio work in many other jobs too. There are many different things to do in the Buckeye State. Because of its beauty, people, land, water, and forests, Ohio is a great place to visit, live, work, and play.

A Cleveland freighter loading coal on the Cuyahoga river.

Fun Facts

•When Ohio became a state in 1803, Chillicothe was the capital. In 1810, the capital moved to Zanesville. Two years later, in 1812, it moved back to Chillicothe. Finally, in 1816, the capital moved to Columbus where it still is today.

•Ohio has more festivals than any other state in the country. Cincinnati's kidfest is the biggest one-day event just for kids.

•In 1966, Carl B. Stokes was elected mayor of Cleveland, Ohio. He was the first African American to lead a big United States city.

•In 1870, two men started major companies in Ohio. Today, more than 100 years later, these two companies are still two of the biggest. Benjamin F. Goodrich started making rubber things at Akron, Ohio. Goodrich Tires is one of his companies. John D. Rockefeller started Standard Oil Company in Cleveland, Ohio.

The birthplace of Thomas Edison.

Glossary

American Revolution: a war that gave the United States its independence from Great Britain.

Border: neighboring states, countries, or waters.

Cattle: farm animals such as cows, bulls, and oxen.

Crops: the big fields of plants where farmers grow corn, beans, or cotton.

Explorers: people that are one of the first to discover and look over land.

Industry: many different types of businesses.

Manufacturing: making a lot of something to sell.

Minerals: things found in the earth, such as rocks, diamonds, or coal.

Miners: people who work underground to get minerals.

Mining: digging underground to get minerals.

Native Americans: the first people who were born in and occupied North America.

Resort: a place to vacation that has fun things to do.

Settlers: people that move to a new land and build a community.

Tourism: an industry that serves people who are traveling for pleasure, and visiting places of interest.

Internet Sites

Civil War Ohio
http://www.iwaynet.net/~lsci/Rbpaper.htm
For Civil War history buffs, find out how Ohio contributed to the war effort. Many military documents as well as old photos and other links are included.

Ohio Festivals, Fairs, Events...
http://www.wcnet.org/~kbrandt/ohio.htm
Your guide to FUN with a great list of Ohio's festivals, fairs, and events. Besides the many links, there are maps, parks, and resorts. Very colorful and fun.

These sites are subject to change. Go to your favorite search engine and type in Ohio for more sites.

PASS IT ON

Tell Others Something Special About Your State

To educate readers around the country, pass on interesting tips, places to see, history, and little known facts about the state you live in. We want to hear from you!
To get posted on ABDO & Daughters website, E-mail us at "mystate@abdopub.com"

Index